I0445457

You Who Are
the Stranger

You Who Are the Stranger: Collected Poems 1979-1989

R. Bremner

WESTBRAE LITERARY GROUP

Copyright © 2025 R. Bremner

All rights reserved. No part of this book may be
reproduced, distributed, or transmitted in any form or
by any means, including photocopying, recording, or
other electronic or mechanical methods, without the
prior written permission of the author, except in the
case of brief quotations embodied in critical reviews
and certain other noncommercial uses permitted by
copyright law.

ISBN: 979-8-9917199-5-7
Published by Westbrae Literary Group
Berkeley, California
Jon-David Hague, Founding Editor

For more information about this and other titles from
Westbrae Literary Group, visit us at
westbraeliterarygroup.com or email us at
info@westbraeliterarygroup.com

For Dr. Francesca Bernadine Dharmakan Bremner,
the lady who makes my life worthwhile

CONTENTS

You try the handle of the road, it opens
Do not be afraid
It's you, my love, you who are the stranger

–Leonard Cohen

Smoke rings like rumors
and dreams like stale cigarettes
in a cracked ashtray left behind
at the old apartment.

A color which I cannot name,
something between mauve and orange,
lingers hardly in layers
over a rambling line of
trees across the bay.
As minutes pass, the trees black-
en, the lower sky hues deepen,
enriched.
Above them a lighter blue, close
to the ocean's, survives, while
the highest sky darkens.

On this side of the highway, the
ocean, still a visible blue, purrs,
audible beneath the steady casual
roar of traffic on Route A1A.

Surfside, Florida, Nov 15, 1981
5:50 - 6:30 PM

Vampires,
our lust divides the
night, splits the side-
walks.
We seep like limp
gas, unknown pores
widen.
You stink of piano keys!
I gorge my dripping
teeth on your noise.
You swallow my brain, and
burp.

This poem is not about actual vampires

Brushstroked rouge swaggers
across the North Florida landscape
captured from an L-1011
at thirty thousand feet.
As day bleeds into night,
the red, now finger-thick,
squeezes softly, its death,
like a life, a suffering
slow blur.

A trial of language

He and his sister were variable antonyms.
Though both counted out their words,
only he tried to spell them.
She believed no tonic speech,
but the loudest of mumbles.

Neither realized the climactic impotence of words
in time.

After the shock of his terse death
she learned the language of gestures.
The parents still do not understand.
They seek words to trust.
We have tried, but
cautious eloquence does not fool them.
She will not talk to them.
She plans to survive.

There are nights when
Sir Roland Hanna's fingers,
so chubby, stubby, and warm,
seem to leave his hands and fly
into icy piano frenzy.

If only my father
hadn't been so damn
RESPONSIBLE.

I want to fly far
from this place.

I want to wake
up to a morning of
unplanned moments and
no duties.
A whole blank day
awaiting my own
script.
A one-man play with
perhaps surprise guest
stars.

But my father was so damn
responsible.

I've known other men who
left their families,
chased beautiful demons
and angels wherever
they led.
Men who would drink all
night if they chose, blow
their pay at the track

or lavish it on friends,
fiends, foes, babes, beasts,
and beauts.

How freeing it must be to
have had a father who
indulged such calls, un-
leashing his son to the
ways and whims of the
world.

But the children of my Dad
never knew how to lack meals
or new clothes every year,
while he made do with old
raglikes from year to year, nor
knew how to miss out on college
while he hammered nails into
roofs in hot sun and cold wind.

But who asked for it? Who
wanted such comfort? Who
told him we wanted him
to suffer for us, our guilt
ever blooming?

Couldn't you have talked it
over with me? Couldn't you
have asked me if you should

be so damn responsible?
For my sake?

The finest poem
I've ever written
was scribbled while Ra-
mona was showering and I
sat in a cathair-drenched
easy chair in her
half a living room while
her three fat, lazy cats
prowled the hot little apart-
ment for cool spots.

Into that poem I invested
all the joy, fear, agony,
mystery, and realization of
a moment in which I
suddenly knew how all
the pieces of life
fit into me in this place, in
this time, now and forever.
The words pulled together a
becalmed, mighty, saved union
of myself and the universe.

I searched and searched
for that poem for many
days, sure that it must
be in my coat pocket or
somewhere near, but
I never saw it after that

day.

Did it somehow get
into that one year's
worth of writing
which I inadvert-
antly threw out in
a stack of old news-
papers one day?

Several times I tried
to recreate that poem but
could not begin to re-
member even the words,
let alone the feeling.

Who knows now if that poem
ever truly existed… or was it
just some psychic metaphor
for my life?

Irina sizzles in time and
space. The air is hot
where she has been. Blonde
blonde hair conceals
the fire that burns
inside her eyes.

BARRACUDA DECISION

The door was locked;
white wine incense
draped the table.
Feeding on our youth,
a supper of wit,
we dined,
occasionally pausing
to say grace beneath the table.

From outside the silver dining room,
echoing off the walls
in the halls of the sterile palace,
computer banjos
spewed rueful tunes
of monogrammed secrecy.
Singular incest
was the rule of the hour
for those who would play the game
properly.
I wanted to play, I think,
(did you?)
till you explained
the player's entry fee
disguised till the final whistle blows.

So go back to chewing your bubblegum
or whatever you do nowadays;
I'll bust open the locked door

with one good strong kick.

for Sylvia Plath

Further thoughts on Phil Ochs, three summers after his passing

Sun files through the pine needles
Bugs filter through the light
Wind tickles the maple leaves.

The light profiles a spider's web,
half torn, which shivers
in the final breeze of summer
as the leaves resume their turning.

ANECDOTE OF THE TWO COYOTES

1) The world received him on a hot stormy night while the dying spring gave convulsed birth to summer.

2) His sun clung stubbornly to Gemini while his moon flirted weakly with distracted Aquarius.

3) His birth was met with the usual fanfare. Relatives tapped the hospital glass. To please his audience, he cooed and clucked and was gratified with their beaming smiles.

4) His mother, aunts and uncles, and teachers oohed and ahhed at his brilliant day-to-day performances.

5) His father and brothers noticed his forced distance from his peers.

6) His mother declared, "This, my brightest son, will become a prominent attorney."

7) Professions and occupations could not stretch far enough to reach him. He sought only to drift on lazy seas and bed the available girls, who were rewarded for their gifts of sighing sentiment by slight glimpses into his wit. He chose a word for himself so that he could not be considered an aimless drifter. The word was "artiste". He walked through this new role with the easy gusto with which he had played his entire life.

8) His writings were summarily dismissed by the important and the unimportant people. This occurred for a number of years.

9) He grew increasingly angry and cynical and shrank mockingly from all vestiges of the literary and intellectual worlds. His works reflected a sharp-honed edge of detachment from every subject or character they touched upon.

10) He was called an "aimless drifter".

11) She was a tall, wispy woman with comfortable eyes that changed color and a loping walk.

12) She was bored with common sense logic, with talkative matter-of-fact people, with self-indulgent dreaming seekers, with being taught what she refused to believe, and with both arguments and the end of them.

13) She sought desperately to write, compose, or create "art", and secretly, flagrantly abused her frustrated ego for her failures while forcibly maintaining a calm, easy exterior.

14) She embraced feminism for release and relief.

15) She made love rarely and laboriously.

16) They met while working in a fast food restaurant.

17) She decided to make him her friend and confidante.

18) He fell immediately, totally, and exultantly in love with her.

19) They made love often, fervently, and unusually.
20) She laughed with him and cried with him.
21) He spoke so often and so certainly of her personal value that she came for the first time to realize it.
22) She fell softly and matter-of-factly in love with him.
23) His writings began to exhibit the wit, style, and grace he had so long and so mistakenly believed were characteristic of everything he did.
24) She consciously let him see that part of her psyche which she believed to be her whole self.
25) He consciously let her see the well-constructed play which he believed to be his whole self.
26) They were casually ecstatic in being together.
27) He became gradually aware of those parts of her into which she had never delved and had therefore never shown him.
28) She became aware that the role he was playing was divorced from though related to its playwright.
29) They became confused, then suspicious, then resentful. He felt betrayed. She felt deceived.
30) Love became difficult. Talk became strained. Empathy became impossible.

31) They parted amicably and tenderly, with few tears and many wishes.

32) She moved in and out of various urban centers, living with various old or new-found friends.

33) She wrote several moderately successful sociological books and sundry articles on contemporary life and its problems.

34) She made love often, passionately, and fiercely.

35) She learned to write excellent poetry which she secreted away from the world as her revenge against it.

36) She fought vicious mental battles with everyone who drew close enough to merit such attention.

37) Her Piscean subconscious became badly and continuously bruised, but she kept the bruises well-hidden under a carefully constructed peaceful exterior, except for those rare occasions when someone tried to draw close to her.

38) She was, over the years, respected as an earnest though misguided critic of society with a volatile but well-meaning temperament. She died in middle age, in relative poverty, of a brain tumor. Her marvelous poems, never discovered, died with her.

39) She had for some time been complaining of irritating voices inside her head, but friends accepted this as one of her lovable eccentricities.

40) He became a computer expert, renting out small portions of his intellect for extravagant sums. Money flooded him, and he stashed away a high percentage, living a bare and barren life.

41) After some years, he packed up his cash and moved into a deep dry cave in an empty, far-removed hill.

42) He survived by eating local vegetation and occasionally feasted on small animals when he could catch them.

43) He took to baying at the moon at odd hours of the morning from a wooded mound.

44) His eyes grew sharp but often seemed to be chuckling. His Aquarius moon was satisfied. His Gemini sun chuckled in acceptance.

Pyrona was always one half-step sadder
than the quickest road to town.
I wed her hoping the shock would shake
the stale dew from her crown.

Now the trees grow dim and the beetle drags
no weight to broaden its track.
I seem to have learned that I am no more
nor less than what I lack.

Pyrona no longer speaks to me
with words I can define,
yet her other voices find a way
to laugh, like wine, with mine.

Raccoons, a story

On those frigid nights, we'd pop up from the subway wind tunnel into the blustery city street, padding past the lamplit haze, chuckling, our blood humming, eager for the ales and the warmth of the table talk.

We'd leave behind a trail of smoky breath, sailing upward and vanishing, vanishing like the breadcrumbs dropped by Hansel and Gretel, vanishing like those theories, those arguments and conjectures, those powerful words and mystical ideas that would soon leap out onto the table before us. So clear, so near, we never thought to try and catch them, to hold and save them. They were there. They would always be there, wouldn't they?

Inside, the black furnace hummed. Our backs snuggled up against its heat, shivers surging the lengths of our spines. Puff-faced and bleary-eyed, we'd speak loudly, forage each other's minds for the food of the soul, that naïve socialist optimism, the camaraderie of intellect and spirit so compatible with good bitter ale.

And as the old man swept the sawdust-covered floor, and the plump cat dozed under the table, we'd pack up our reassured faiths, gather our torn coats and years of rich promise, and set ourselves for the long dark cold path to the subway.

How little we understood then of the greyish smoke of our ale-worn words, so easily seized and muted by the cold darkness of the night around us.

My father walks
with head bowed down.
He never trips
on buckled sidewalks
and oftentimes
he finds lost coins.

I resolved
early on
to tilt my head
slightly upward
while I walk.
I think I see
much more than he
but I often trip
and seldom find
lost coins.

This situation is a projection
of the repetition of certain images
in your mind.

These images were born to facts
which died, and were adopted
by rumor, taught by conjecture,
and given self-awareness by
your own awakening mental
resources.

Or so I think.
What's your guess?

All these absurd rules
I've never understood
now begin to make sense
seen through the bottom
of an empty beer mug.

They lace into a soft but strong net
stretching out below you
to catch your helpless falling body
and bounce you back up again.

You are saved from the terror,
the strange fate of falling
faultlessly free to some unknown
and doubtless horrible destination -
if there be an end to the fall at all.

JC has found religion, a poem in four parts

The Symbionese Liberation Army, more by its verve
than by its minimal bloody success
has given Christina hope anew;
at least she seemed pleased
speaking fervently of her matriarchal communism
beneath the elevated tracks of the Harrison PATH train,
she looking far too pale and thin,
but lovely as ever nonetheless.
With prodding she admitted concern
for the pain and death in the SLA revelries,
though not for the stolen hard-earned bucks
of hard-working cab drivers like myself.

The shock of intersecting in this manner
with my long-unseen counter-culture dreamgirl
fortunately did not leave me speechless.

The jobless time in Seattle has not been good
for Chris.
She's two years older and two years behind
where she should be; no one is writing
psychedelic feminism anymore.
Her once-snug jeans now struggle to stay up,
but to me, she's still quite unmatched.
But far more crucial than all this of loves lost
and new-bought dreams
is the arrival of my train above,
for Truffaut awaits at the Bleecker Street Cinema.
Day for Night gobbles all smaller matters
when it comes to play in town again.
(1976)

Billy Joe has positioned the piano carefully
in the corner where, if he squeezes past the pingpong table,
he can reach it, but playing is painful in these poor acoustics.

Pip's Lounge no longer keeps a piano, and so
Billy Joe prepares to enter a programming school
following in my profitable footsteps
as fulltime pragmatist and part-time poet.

He will play his beautiful melodies upon the 370/145
and, I still pray, before attentive crowds someday.
(1979)

Margie phones me late at night, though we have nothing to say.
She needs to hear me pick it up, and I need to hear it ring,
she still not realizing that we'll never meet again.
The brownest eyes and fullest breasts I've ever seen
are just as brown and full, at least in the honest memories.
But in the desperate, gasping escape from a past
of self-torture, despair, and her, my greatest failure,
there was no time to free the love and take it with me.
(1979)

JC does not pick apples in Washington State anymore.
He does not drive the #6 bus through the Lincoln Tunnel.
He no longer seeks Brother Maurice to sign
forms designating him a conscientious objector.
He does not hitch rides from me on Schuyler Ave,
Nor run across me at the Ridge Lounge.
He does run occasionally at Garrett Mountain.
It brings him closer to his Lord,

(28)

as does living again in his mother's house.
John Cain has found religion, or rather
the Church has nudged with its rugged staff
one more innocent crying lamb
back into the tendered fold.
(1979)

We wanted so much to change the world.
We had the plans to change the world.
We had a need to save the world.
But the world didn't want
Or need that saving.

Stopping by whores on a crowded street

Whose whores these are I think I know.
His home is in the Village though;
He will not see me stopping here
To watch his whores fill up with dough.

My little cab must think it queer
To stop without a red light near
'Tween bums and junkies on the make
The hottest evening of the year.

It gives the engine quite a shake
To ask if there is some mistake.
The only other sound's the sweep
Of pimps a-counting up their take.

The whores are lovely, dark and deep.
But I have promises to keep,
And bucks to earn before I sleep,
And bucks to earn before I sleep.

with apologies to Robert Frost and the ladies of Tenth
Avenue

The crossing of the Red Sea

The sky is a red sea,
The moon is a smooth stone.
Dark cloud eroding islands
Shade deep-hung cliffs.

Washed in by such an evening tide:
Revolutions gasp in bartered currents;
Romance erodes in dullish sweat;
Creation skims and dips away.

But in the cleaven sea, something
bright excites the iris.
And the cool, round moon echoes
with remembered melodies.
And in the dark island caves
lurking, hiding,
waiting to be discovered,
lives…what promise?
  what fate?

These are reasons;
fair enough,
as reasons go.
No less real
than any abstract.
No less false
than any trust.

The sky is a red sea,
The moon is a smooth stone.
Dark cloud ferry steamers
Pledge to carry me home.

billets of clouds
in regimental array
fanning out stealthily:

quiet, efficiency, surprise.
awaiting word
from command post

they fill the sky
take it
and hold it

without resistance.

Sleep

As smooth fog
in silken wisps of smoke
a gently heaving lover floats
in the soft romance of sleep.

Still ardor, bliss serene,
rapture for the tired hand.
Reward in passionate retreat
when life's demanding voice
quiets for a succinct spell.

In Paterson, at Blimpies
sit Aristotle and Descartes
at a plastic table
in plastic chairs
watching through the blue plate glass
for their bus to Fair Lawn
while outside in the slush mess
stands a huddle of shiverers
waiting too.
And "Aw, shuddup!" says Aristotle.
"NO, you shuddup!" says Descartes.
The giggle frantically in
appreciation of each other's wit.
Meanwhile at the back table
sits Sigmund Freud carefully
tempering his coffee with cream,
studying intensely the play
being acted out before him
while Holden Caulfield sweeps the floor.
And "Aw, shuddup!" says Aristotle.
"NO, you shuddup!" says Descartes.
After many shuddups
the Fair Lawn bus arrives.
Aristotle and Descartes
guffaw frantically, fraternally
as they charge through Blimpies door
while Sigmund, unsmiling still,
sips his weak brew
and outside the cream pours onto the bus

(35)

and inside Holden sweeps Blimpies floor.

This concerns an actual incident in 1979, when I was a student at ECPI on Market Street in Paterson, New Jersey. One winter's day I was sitting in in the "Blimpie Base" at Main and Market, wasting time before my Main Line train back to Passaic, when the incident unfolded.

Rimbaud: last letter to Verlaine

My dearest Paul,

   As now the scorching fires in my leg
will not desist (perhaps foreshadowing
my eternal fate), my mind aches too, with
thoughts of you, as sometime last night,
or the time I acquaint with last
night, as my hours have no distinction
now, the Saviour came to raise me from
this bed of hell, but lo! His Face was
yours, and I cried out, slipping through
His grasp back into Hell.
   For those days are long past, those
days of foolish whimsey, staggering through
the streets under singing stars. And you,
my love, scavenger of my morbid moods,
defiler of my sacred youth, whose soul did
I torrefy to see the flames not of Hell but
of a glorious Heaven, the Heaven of you, to
you I must account so many years.
My pale, tender skin once cringed from
the sweltering heat of Paris, my protection
from burning being angels of the Lord (your-
self one), whose dreaming rhymes my own
pursued. But how cold grew Paris, my wretched
body a frozen lake with only the alcohol in my
bloodstream to keep the deeper waters flowing.

Sick from staggering, from shivers, and from vomit, sick of your postured holy platitudes so defenseless against my debaucheries, like the rosary you dropped, trembling, before my nakedness, and sick of passion so wearying to maintain, with its fitful madness and violent bursts,

I sought my peace in the fortunes of the warm East, my agile mind a productive machine. No more torn pockets for a poor lad, this former lamb became a thriving merchant. No drunken boats carry me now, no lyric muses touch my eyes, or caress my senses with their soft beauty. Sweating in the steaming cities of Africa, my heart was becalmed. But never have I felt so cold as now, on return to Marseilles. No amount of coverings can keep the fearful cold away.

I hear the silken voice of God, a God Who is not you, Paul. Let us neither curse the foul deeds we wrought upon each other's psyches, nor moan for our former ecstasies, but deliver ourselves into His Hands, Who raised your arm when you shot at me, sending me on my journey to His doorstep today.

The ghost chaser

He chased a ghost
to the crack of our whip.
Our simple plan:
the ghost would vaporize
through his fingers
before delighted eyes
and excited sighs.
The stupid man!
He couldn't understand
the plan.
He caught the ghost
we loved the most.
His prize:
the stings of our whip.
Away he ran.

for Roger Maris

Scamp

There's pleasure in that big body,
(which nobody, least of all I, can deny)
lurking impishly
in every inch
of that unquestionably
deliciously ample flesh.
What eyes! To say that they
sparkle, flash, flicker, or burn
would only serve to paint her
on your brain like oil on canvas,
but listen!
Those eyes, those eyes press their
impression into me, a delicate
yet firm pressure, with the tickling
lashes (promising or only teasing, I
never could distinguish)
an invitation to discover
the scamp she longs
so desperately
to take such pleasure in being.

My memories are little men
with pad and pencil sitting
in my ear, reviewing notes
to remind me of my agony, when
starving, I crawled through
lush green fronds

into a garden so plentiful,
all cool and damp,
with ripe fruits drooping
down the branches
of their overburdened trees,
and my tears welled up,
oh, so full were my eyes
with tears of gratitude for my
splendid deliverance,
till suddenly I discovered with horror
that my lips were sewn shut.

Sewn shut by the mouthful
who stands,
so self-assuredly glorious in
her prim, sexual plumpness,
so near, so
frustratingly unable to
see in my eyes the
recognition of the
scrumptiousness she
is praying to God that my
mouth will water for once more.

This sweet young thing
of the clenched fist breasts
dreams mightily of medio-
crity prostrate on an altar
before her eager knife; dubs
brightness the beloved eunuch
cherished, friend but never
ever to be desired; all
the don't knows and never'd
guesses shimmy through her shivers
but brightness drools, hungrily
lusting denied melons,
not even satisfied
with understanding.

Hazy, Dazy,
Dole me your anisette.
I've seemed crazy
All for the things you wet.
Don't hope for a stylized kaddish;
We can't afford such parish.
But we'll find heat
In sundry suites
When our synergy melts
All debt.

Blue

Blue,
      blue,
            blue is my love,
              present of the rise,
Vanishing quickly like the dove
              falling through the skies.

Blue,
      blue,
            blue is my love,
              waking in the breeze,
Humming as she fades above
              her thousand reveilles.

Blue,
      blue,
            blue is my love,
              stolen by the rise,
Humming as she fades above
              her thousand lullabies.

art is the last refuge of scoundrels
love is the lost refuge of fools
sex is the antiseptic for festering wounds
poetry is the weakest excuse of losers
and the triumphant gloat of winners.

Though you're not yet here,
my thoughts are not of
anticipation of you, but
rather of the quiet aftertaste
of your kisses, and
the cool electricity that
 lingers when you leave.

The still magic you crowd about
has found me once again.
A spark and a wash
in the gushing air
creep and tuck
through all the fear
as all that we know
seems to hush, and hide
for just one very fine moment
or two.

amoral movements:
hair brushed
from a perfect cheek;
auburn sunset
weeping for bygone
cloud cover

luscious
spiraling blonde curls
devastating firm
vicious beauty

Mailer

To be on everyone's tongue
at the parties;
to showcase every fool's dry wit;
to provide high school English teachers
with anecdotes;

You must have had more purpose
in life than this, Mailer.

You are quite like the old
boxer George Chuvalo,
bloodied, weary, but always battling,
lacking the knockout punch,
but forever game, tough to bring down,
(hardest head of them all -
hurts their fists)
never running from the punishment
from better fighters...

So why do they cheer your opponents so,
and why do you chase
every fan from your corner?

Sometimes, when I'm riding the #74 bus
into Paterson in the morning, with the bleary-eyed
bus people, and as a surpassingly lovely black girl
in white hospital getup takes a seat near the front
and munches her breakfast of sour cream and
onion flavored potato chips, and then onto the bus
steps a dark- haired white beauty with perfect deep
brown eyes and perfect lashes and perfect cheeks,
in a beige trenchcoat and gripping an issue of
Cosmopolitan and, surveying the many empty
seats, selects the one directly in front of me, her
brown-black hair painstakingly perfectly frizzed to
give the appearance of not having been worked on
at all, lapping slightly over the metal bar on the
back of her seat with the early spring sun shining
from the east through the window on the other
side of the bus, I get that feeling again, that
California feeling, and I'm back up in the dunes
on the beach in San Francisco on one of those
windy overcast days, or else I'm walking and
watching the summer sun set over the ocean,
maybe stopping to sketch the outline of some
sweet young thing sitting on the stone wall
watching the sun set, and I'm feeling oh, how I
could write were I there now, what glorious and
magnificent poetic expression would come
pouring out of me, but here I am on the #74 and
who's to say that Miss Potato Chips and Cosmo
are not as real as the dunes and the sweet young

thing on the wall and all? Cosmo's perfect 1978
hair is there in front of me and I begin to become
aware that a certain part of my anatomy could
begin to strongly appreciate her proximity, and I
realize that this is quite possibly her daily
intention, in various guises and disguises, and the
thought comes to me that this intention, whether
conscious or not, is what makes being on this bus
so perverse. So I turn my gaze to the White Castle
hamburger joint outside, unpeopled at this hour,
and after awhile two teen girls hop onto the bus,
the second a blonde who can't be more than
fourteen, but she's already got a waist, and the
jeans define her quite efficiently, so I give her the
obligatory lick of the lips and she smirks back in
appreciation, and I realize that now without my
moustache I can pass for eighteen, wow, what a
trip, while in front of me Cosmo sighs and I'm
grateful that at least no one on the bus is smoking
for a change. Onto the bus now steps an auburn-
haired sweetie in a long skirt and she sits right
next to Cosmo, in front of me, and Auburn has
hair that is generally straight but fluffed a bit in
front, of the style that was all the universal rage
three years ago but has died out now, and it's
pretty, but nothing close to perfection like
Cosmo's, and she turns sideways and has such a
nice face, though again not nearly so perfect as
Cosmo's, so I have to say hello to Auburn and we

talk and her voice is tasty like a tangerine and even Cosmo joins in happily, but after only a few blocks Auburn is gone before I can ask for her number and now I sink back and Cosmo and I don't talk and I know she's harboring some great amount of venom for me because I gave Auburn the attention which I wouldn't give to her and I am grateful for having had the chance to, and satisfied for having paid tribute to Auburn at her expense. So now I pull the buzzer and hand the driver the ticket and exchange take it easys and get off, and the day has gone so unexpectedly well so far, and ahead is the store on Market Street where I'll pause and stare at the Olivetti and the electric Smith Corona typewriters in the window for as long as the clock will allow before moving about my obligatory business.

Carl
can sleep a free
man again,
those unmentionable
sighs of thought beaten
and banished.
Demons were at the door
last night
but he turned out the lights
and hid.

Like brown, withered leaves
scattered in shimmering winds,
beliefs drift away.

Fresh, warm-smelling grass
sparkling with heavy wetness
bows slowly, stiffly.

Slithering black shapes
dance moonlight ceiling dances
in my room at night.

White wine, rock and roll.
Phone calls, street rap, gnats, and heat.
It's a sort of life.

Clouds between the trees
like Monet haystacks,
but paler
seem almost tender
from the hospital window
on the day of her spinal tap
as she hums
into the pillow:

get your ribbons on, honey
get your ribbons on
we gonna rock, honey
all night long.

Here by the twist in the brook
the rest of the world seems obsolete;
but I know in my silenced heart
it is the brook, and I, which are.

The Pearl

The feint,
The spin,
The lurch,
The score.

The charge,
The trip.

The lunge,
The steal,
The pass,
Two more.

The shove,
The slip.

The rhythm
The flow,
The jerk,
The whirl.
The frenzy,
The cheers,
The magic,
The Pearl.

for Earl "The Pearl" Monroe

decision against suicide

I can't die now.
There are those three poems to type up.

Fourth of July

Washington DC, July 4, 1985.
400 North Capitol Street, NW.
6th floor on the Amtrak side of
the building, not the C-SPAN side.

Prowling the aisles. Passing
the hours. Desk after empty
desk.

9:30 AM, a beautiful sunny day.
Pressed against a window pane
I can almost but not quite see
the Mall, which will fill in the
afternoon with friends, lovers,
and families swarming for the
concert.

Thank God Roy's was open this
morning for breakfast. That
homeless guy was there asking
the manager for a job again,
getting the same story again,
borrowing my Washington Post and
discussing the sports news again.

Also that tattered dress old
woman who buys a cup of coffee

and battles for multiple free
refills every day. Sometimes
she gets them, God bless her.
Depends on who's at the counter
and what kind of day they've had.

Especially good to hear those two
today.

At 12:30, lunch at the American
Cafe with my well paid French
escort. She won't eat but will
have a drink with me before
a picnic with her French expatriate
friends. I'll Metro back to the
office.

Like the Age of Aquarius, there's
no place for emotion in the Age
of Reagan.

Back at the office, there are more
hours to waste.

The night will be better than
the day.
Thank God tomorrow's a real
day.

The day after Halloween,
1986, Hermosa
Beach, California, USA

A wild-haired lad pedals down the
pavement to the beach,
leaning and weaving this
way and that.
A calico cat snoozes
lustily
on a wooden step to a beach house
on 18th Street.
There are no black cats to be
found today.
A huge pumpkin lies smashed
on concrete, flies like so
much pepper upon the wet
rinds unmoving, as if drawing
recuperative medicine from
the flopping threads and
scattered seeds.

The lad pedals past the
symbol of yesterday.

The sky is grey, the air
too cool for
 November in Southern
California.

(65)

No ghosts, no witches,
no goblins about, just
beach locals and a
few misplaced city folk
gathering for Corona beers
outside Miguel's Burrito
House,

ready to start the
real trick or
treating of a
windy week's
end,

while I wander with
my camera searching
for some truth to
push me through the
winding path of
another month in
exile.

wear the black shoes
out the back door
on the muddy path
to the shack.

Into the cuckoo clock I run
a man of sorts
a machine of course
the exercise of a stronger mind
or the fantasy of a weaker mind?

Here is the clock I've just begun
zooming through the queerest hours
discovering my most frightening powers
your screams of course
my dreams endorse
in throbs of a great black pulsing sun

The clock won't strike
The door is locked
My way is blocked
The tick like a clicking set of teeth
quickens my blood while the blackness seethes
and here I stay
I find my way
the
clock
won't
strike

Recipe

First, gather to you every bit of accumulated knowledge,
every particle of experience, every hard lesson learned
along the road of humanity.
Toss them in a bowl and mix with strong, swift strokes.

With a sharp blade, scrape from your skin
the dirt and grime of every failure,
the sweat of frustration, the bruises of despair.
Into the bowl with them.

Then stretch both arms deep down your throat.
Scratch and grope for every grit, every scrap of compassion,
of love, of fear, of misery, of hate.
Into the bowl.

Cover and shake violently
till contents come smooth and silky.

The pour the mixture out on the ground.
You have thus cleaned and sterilized the bowl;
now you are ready to begin the recipe.

The roundness, first.

At contrast to the stark, harsh
thin-lined spires straining
to a restless heaven.
Alien to the demand
of the hard-honed cannon.

Then a relaxation into
revelation of the calm,
the steady, the easy push.

All things flow from
the rhythmic warmth beneath, and
the mind rocks with tender excitement,
fueled on by remembrance of
anticipation heartily satisfied:
the stirring melody,
sweet scent,
and luscious taste
of a life.

But first, the roundness.

Snowflakes,
messengers of quiet death
emerge from sheaths of white sky
to visit the dry-spotted window.
It's a careless death they promise,
to be neither welcomed nor feared,
when faces I watched grow firm and strong
have melted softly like the snow.

I belong with them,
with the white of the flakes
and their murky living sky.

The only sadness seems that those
who now agree I've lived too long
will weep sincerely when I've gone.

If any of them could hear now
my voice gone silent beneath the pane
I'd tell them through the clean white sheet:

Mourn not for what was once and is not now,
but for what is and should not be.

headlights

shield a passion
under glassed sighs

and eyes that dart
to the road and from

Smash the mirror.
Smash the clock.
Smash the windows.
Break the door.

Cut your fingers
on broken pieces.
Pick them up
to rearrange.

Kill the image
Kill the dream.
Kill the vision.
Break the spell.

Today wears tomorrow's mask
and yesterday's gloves

closing its eyes
pretending to dream

while the hands work overtime
racking up to the time and a half

shaving off the questions,
carving the lies

all the time protected
by the rugged gloves.

There is more truth in the mask

Than in all the agonizingly
over-perfectly sculpted monuments
it leaves behind.

An illusion of thunder
high up in the sky
shaking the sturdy earth
unsettling stringy shadows
before fading in a whisper
in grey horizons
leaving rich memories
as if it ever was.

Class of '67.
Clean the eye.
Finish the jigsaw puzzle
before the rain
warps the pieces.
Write down brave words
if there are any
if any come to mind
if you dare.
Wait patiently.
Pieces of piano.
The best and the brightest.
What the hell
is goin' on?
They were only
the best and the brightest.
It's almost over.
They all wore skirts then.
The knees looked better.
Maybe the paper faded,
defeated them.
Maybe it was deliberate
cosmic betrayal.
Winding slide guitar.

They were only
the best and the brightest
because we don't remember right,
because we were stupid then about

what matters.

College radio stations, 1981.
But it's not midnight again.
Don't "live with me".
Stones.
Finish the puzzle.
Before.
It all.
And the rains drip,
and the eye is washed clean.

for Monk, Gua, Patti, Ray, Joby and Queen Kathy and her
court and the rest of the Class of '67

Acknowledgements

"A trial of language," *International Poetry Review*, Fall 1983

"The Crossing of the Red Sea," *Passaic Review*, 1979

"In Paterson, at Blimpies," *Paterson Literary Review*, 2015

"Hazy Dazy," *The Quarterday Review*, Spring 2016

"Scamp," *The Gambler*, March 11, 2016

"Brushstroked rouge swaggers," *Panoply*, April 2016

"Rimbaud: last letter to Verlaine," *Panoply*, August 2016

"Barracuda Decision," *Poets Online*, July 2013

"Anecdote of the Two Coyotes," *The Offbeat/Quirky Anthology*, June 2017

"There are nights," *Jerry Jazz Musician*, May 19, 2017

"The Ghost Chaser," *Great Falls Festival Anthology*, May 1979; and *Spitball Magazine*, September 2013

"Stopping by Whores on a Crowded Street," *The Journal of Formal Poetry*, Spring 2015

"Raccoons," *Every Writer's Resource*, *Flash Boulevard*, and *A la carte*

"Sleep," *Mensa Bulletin*, no. 228, July/August 1979

"A color which I cannot name," *The Poet*, 'On the Road' issue, August 2020

About the Author

R. Bremner writes of incense, peppermints, and the color of time in such venues as International Poetry Review, Anthem: a Leonard Cohen Tribute Anthology, Poets Online, Jerry Jazz Musician, Paterson Poetry Review, Passaic Review, Yellow Chair Review, Adelaide Literary Magazine, Peacock Journal, Oleander Review, Shot Glass Journal, Climate of Opinion: Sigmund Freud in Poetry, and others.

His careers included stints as cab driver, security guard, truck unloader, computer programmer for Pan American World Airways, and bank vice-president.

He appeared in the first issue of the Passaic Review, an issue to which Allen Ginsberg also contributed.

Ron has published seven books of poetry with "outlaw" and small presses, including Absurd (Cajun Mutt Press) and Hungry words (Alien Buddha Press), and 13 unpublished books superior to those published. He has thrice won Honorable Mention in the Allen Ginsberg awards, and he invites you to visit his Instagram poetry at beat_poet1.

He has featured at the prestigious Bowery Poetry Club in New York's East Village, and at the ANT Bookstore, Montclair Library, Paterson Poetry Festival, Paterson Library, Gallery U, Brownstone Poets, Creativity Caravan, and elsewhere.

He lives with his beautiful sociologist wife, son, and dog Ariel in wonderful Northeast New Jersey.

www.ingramcontent.com/pod-product-compliance
Lightning Source LLC
Chambersburg PA
CBHW020758130626
46554CB00006B/2245